12·6·2011

EXTREME ENVIRONMENTAL THREATS™

ENDANGERED WILDLIFE

Habitats in Peril

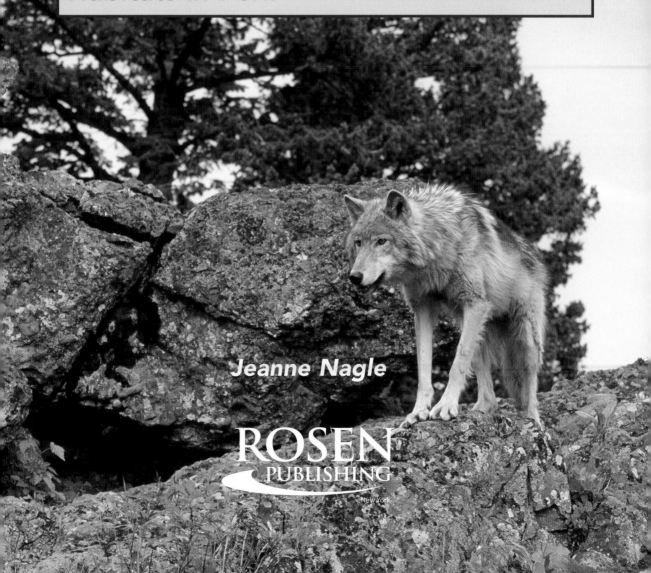

Jeanne Nagle

ROSEN
PUBLISHING

New York

Published in 2009 by The Rosen Publishing Group, Inc.
29 East 21st Street, New York, NY 10010

Library of Congress Cataloging-in-Publication Data

Nagle, Jeanne.
Endangered wildlife : habitats in peril / Jeanne Nagle.—1st ed.
        p. cm.—(Extreme environmental threats)
Includes bibliographical references and index.
ISBN-13: 978-1-4358-5019-4 (library binding)
ISBN-13: 978-1-4358-5375-1 (pbk)
ISBN-13: 978-1-4358-5379-9 (6 pack)
1. Endangered species—Juvenile literature. 2. Endangered ecosystems—Juvenile literature. 3. Wildlife conservation—Juvenile literature. 4. Habitat conservation—Juvenile literature. I. Title.
QL83.N34 2009
333.95'416—dc22

                                                            2008016586

Manufactured in Malaysia

On the cover: Polar bears are considered to be a threatened species by the United States, though most environmentalists and many nations consider them endangered (a more urgent threat level requiring greater species protections). Polar bears are threatened by a variety of factors, including climate change, hunting, habitat loss, interaction with humans, and oil drilling. **Title page:** A wolf roams its rocky habitat in Yellowstone National Park.

Contents

INTRODUCTION

Since 1980, nearly 112 species of frogs have disappeared from habitats around the world. Climate change and disease are two reasons why.

The world's wildlife is vanishing at an alarming rate. Scientists at the Nature Conservancy and the World Wildlife Federation estimate that one in four mammals, and a full third of Earth's amphibians, such as frogs, are in danger of no longer existing, or becoming extinct. Even wild animals that are not expected to face extinction may very well experience a massive decline in their populations. Even though new species, or types, of animals are discovered every year, extinction numbers keep climbing. In fact, scientists who study

wildlife believe that some animals are becoming extinct before they can be officially recorded as a species. They're gone without anyone ever knowing they existed in the first place.

Reduced numbers of certain species of animals is actually a normal occurrence caused by a process known as natural selection. You might have heard it called "survival of the fittest." Weaker species that consistently lose the battle for food and territory eventually die off and become extinct.

Natural extinction is usually a slow process, happening to a few individual species over the course of about a million years. According to members of the prestigious American Institute of Biological Sciences, however, hundreds of wildlife species around the globe are currently fighting for their survival—and often losing. Species are becoming extinct at a rate that is anywhere from one hundred to one thousand times faster than normal. A loss that big and quick would create a mass extinction equal to or greater than the one scientists believe wiped out the dinosaurs sixty-five million years ago.

Nature alone has not sped up the rate of extinction. More threats to the well-being and survival of wild animals come from human sources. People have been in fierce competition with wild animals for land, food, and natural resources for years. Humans have usually proven themselves the stronger species in this battle. When overhunting and overfishing of species and a rise in the level of pollution are added to this mix, humans come to represent the single gravest threat to wildlife survival.

The truly scary thing is that it's not just wildlife that is threatened by the possibility of species extinction. Animals of all shapes and sizes provide ecological services such as restoring soil or filtering and cleansing water. Any species that disappears leaves a hole in the web of life. Mass extinction would leave so many holes that the web might totally fall apart.

Humans may be able to undo some of the damage they inflict on wildlife. They can do this through conservation efforts. The most important thing they can do, however, is realize the important role wildlife plays in the survival of the planet—before it's too late.

Habitats are places where wildlife can safely live. Some wild animals gather together in groups known as herds, packs, or flocks for protection.

Throughout the past fifty years or so, humans have spent a great deal of time and money exploring other planets and outer space, trying to figure out whether we are alone in the universe. The truth is, we're not alone even here on Earth. Humans share the planet and its resources with hundreds, even thousands, of animal species.

Some of these species have been domesticated, or trained to live in a human-controlled environment. In North America, pets such as cats and dogs are the most common domesticated animals. What we call livestock, which are farm and working animals, are also considered domesticated. Then there are animals that live in the wild, with little or no interaction with humans. As a group, we call these creatures wildlife.

CLASS AND SPECIES

More than one million types of wildlife have been identified and named throughout the world. In order to study them, it would be helpful to break them down into smaller groups. Luckily, science has already taken care of that. Each and every living thing on Earth can be divided into scientific categories. The categories get smaller and more specific as they go along.

Whether they are domesticated or wild, animals are considered either vertebrates (with spines) or invertebrates (without spines). Insects are an example of the invertebrate class. Vertebrates are broken down into smaller groups called mammals, birds, fish, reptiles, and amphibians. Each of these smaller categories is separated further into species, which are individual varieties of animals within each larger class.

Animals within a species have many physical and behavioral traits in common. Similar physical traits include the way animals look, their size, their life expectancy (how long they are expected to live), and

Fido's and Fluffy's Wild Past

Today's domesticated animals started out as wildlife. For instance, dogs are believed to be descended from wolves that grew to trust and live with humans. House cats are believed to be the domestic version of wild cats that roamed the Middle East nearly ten thousand years ago and still live there today. In fact, most pets and livestock can trace their roots to ancestors that lived apart from humans but eventually came to depend on people for basic necessities. These include food, water, shelter, and protection from disease and other threats to their survival.

how they give birth. Behaviors that are alike in a species include the way animals hunt, the type of food they eat, how they mate, and how they interact with other creatures in general.

NO PLACE LIKE HOME

One of the things that all species have in common is their need for a suitable habitat, or a place to live. A wildlife habitat is a section of wilderness that provides plenty of food, water, and shelter, as well as room to grow and socialize. For it to be a workable, sustaining habitat, the area must remain in its natural state, untouched by human activity. That means people should

Quiet, relatively undisturbed places are the preferred habitats of wild creatures. For instance, these ibises make their home in the Outer Banks region of North Carolina.

not live or work there, and even visiting the area should be kept to a minimum, so as not to disturb the wildlife.

Habitats are communities where animals of the same species live together in groups known as populations. These populations exist within larger ecosystems, which are geographic areas defined by their unique climates (long-term weather patterns), soil and air quality, water availability, and environments, or overall surroundings. Ecosystems can be terrestrial, meaning on land, or aquatic, which means in water. Forests, deserts, prairies, oceans, rivers, and lakes are among the areas that are considered ecosystems.

Wild animals live in habitats that will best support them. For example, herbivores, which are plant eaters, need to live in a place where there is plenty of vegetation. Animals that eat meat, on the other hand, don't need as many plants around. They need to live in a place that has creatures they can hunt and kill for food.

While different populations can and do exist in the same ecosystem, two different species cannot share a habitat. The area would be too small for more than one species, and the competition for food, space, and other resources would eventually result in one of the groups being driven from the habitat.

If something happens to change a habitat—say, the water dries up or is suddenly undrinkable, or another species takes over a large section of land for its own use—one of two things will occur. Either the animal will leave the area in search of a more suitable habitat, or it will adapt to its changed surroundings.

ADAPTATION

Adapting means to get used to something or change so that a given situation better fits your needs. It is sort of nature's way of "going with the flow." There are two basic forms of adaptation: structural and behavioral. Structural adaptation happens at the genetic level, where the physical characteristics of a creature change. This usually takes place slowly and over a long period of time. The shape or size of a bird's beak or mammal's paw is an example of a structural adaptation.

Many different species have changed or evolved in a way that increases their chances of survival in their natural habitat. Polar bears have thick fur and snowshoe-like paws, and penguins have an extra layer of fat so that they can live in the icy cold of the Arctic (North Pole) and Antarctica (South Pole), respectively. Likewise, the thorny devil lizard has tiny grooves in its skin that capture water from rain and dew, which it then channels to its mouth and drinks by making a gulping motion. That's a handy adaptation to have in the hot, dry desert, which is the thorny devil's habitat.

Animals are able to adapt their behavior much more quickly than it takes them to go through structural adaptation. Behavioral adaptations don't require waiting several generations—or even thousands of years—for wildlife's physical characteristics to change. Instead, they are actions that animals have either learned from others in their habitat, from their own experience, or by instinct, which means they are motivated to act a certain way from birth. One example of behavioral adaptation is the hunting patterns of lions in Africa. They spend

Adaptations let animals make the best of their environmental situations. Horned devils are able to find water even in the middle of a desert.

most of the day sleeping in the shade in order to save their energy and keep out of the blazing sun. They hunt in the early morning, when it's still cool, and they do so as a group.

Conserving, or saving, energy and traveling in groups are common themes when it comes to behavioral adaptations. Hibernation involves going into a deep, sleeplike state, where an animal's body temperature gets lower and its heart rate and breathing slow way down. Some animals, such as black bears, live off stored body fat during hibernation, while others wake up every few days or weeks to eat food they've collected beforehand. This behavioral adaptation helps wildlife stay safe and warm during the winter months, when it is harder to hunt and there is less food available. It allows them to save precious energy that would otherwise be hard to replenish with a severely limited food supply.

Migration is when groups of animals temporarily move to a habitat that has better food, shelter, and/or

Geese and other birds migrate to warm locations during the cold winter months. Sanctuaries, such as the one pictured above in India, are favorite migratory gathering spots.

climate. Several species of birds and fish migrate in the fall, seeking warmer weather. In the spring, they return to their normal habitat. Many migrating animals, such as geese, travel in groups to guard against predators and to make the trip easier. Zoologists, or scientists who study animals, believe that birds migrate by instinct, driven by inborn changes that occur in their bodies and brains. They rely on the sun, moon, stars, and Earth's magnetic field to help them navigate to their destination.

WILDERNESS SURVIVAL TECHNIQUES

Adaptations don't just allow wildlife to exist in their habitats. Sometimes, being able to adapt is a matter of life or death. For instance, the structural adaptation known as camouflage lets an animal blend in with its environment. This makes it hard for predators to hunt and kill it for food. In the case of some large predators, such as polar bears, which are white like the ice and snow of their habitat, camouflage makes it easier for them to hunt because they can better sneak up on their prey.

Mimicry is another structural adaptation that works in a similar fashion. To mimic is to copy or imitate, so mimicry is when an animal has physical characteristics that fool predators into thinking it is stronger, nastier, or otherwise better able to defend itself than it actually is. An example scientists frequently point to is the viceroy butterfly, which is completely edible but has colors and patterns on its wings that make it look like a monarch butterfly, which apparently tastes awful. Predators are often fooled and won't eat the viceroy.

THE IMPORTANCE OF BIODIVERSITY

Imagine a world where there was only one type of person, one way of doing things, day in, day out. Not only would life be pretty boring, but many of the necessary

Thanks to their white fur and snowshoe-like paws, polar bears are built to survive in their arctic habitat.

elements of a happy, healthy life would be lost. That's because each experience enriches our lives, and each individual plays a role in making the world a productive and meaningful place. In much the same way, various types of wildlife, with each creature doing what it does best, are required to keep an ecosystem alive and healthy.

Scientists refer to the variety of life on Earth as biological diversity, or biodiversity for short. This term applies to diversity, or differences, at several levels: among species, within species because of their genes, and among various ecosystems. In other words, even though they may have some characteristics in common, each species, each individual within a species, and the environments of each ecosystem are unique and different from one another.

Biodiversity is a hot topic these days when talking about wildlife. Scientists are tremendously concerned that losing species will upset the balance that biodiversity brings to an ecosystem. A lack of balance greatly affects the quality of life for all living things—including humans, as will be examined in the next chapter.

VALUABLE, VITAL, FRAGILE

Killing animals for their skins was a primary way to make money in early America. Native Americans sometimes helped fur trappers conduct their business.

Throughout history, the roles wildlife has played on the planet have been as complex and varied as the species themselves. Wild animals have been objects of worship, revered by various cultures for their religious and spiritual significance. They have been a valuable commodity and major source of income for early North American settlers, who sold wild animal furs so that wealthy Europeans could have fashionable hats and coats. Wildlife has also been misunderstood as some-thing dangerous that needed to be tamed, mastered, or destroyed, while their natural habitats were often viewed as a roadblock to building and "progress."

Today, some of these approaches to wildlife still apply in various parts of the world. However, we also have come to a better understanding of wildlife as a valuable resource, a vital contributor to a healthy environment, and part of a fragile web of life that includes all living things on Earth.

MUTUALISM

Each ecosystem is a study in cooperation. Animals in the wild are interdependent, meaning they depend on each other to survive. Within each ecosystem, there are several examples of different species of wildlife interacting with and supporting each other, for the benefit of all. This is a concept known as mutualism.

In the world's oceans, pilot fish get nutrition from the parasites that attach themselves to sharks. They have even been known to feed off scraps of food that get caught in the shark's teeth. Because of this interaction, the sharks get rid of annoying parasites—and they get a cleaner smile. In return, the pilot fish get not only a meal but, as long as they stick close to the sharks, protection from predators. Several land animals experience a similar relationship with birds. Elephants, hippopotamuses, and other grazing animals frequently have insects buzzing around them. Birds will ride and swoop around the beasts, eating the insects. The birds get fed, and the mammals are rid of annoying pests.

Animals in the wild frequently help each other live more comfortably. Birds and large grazing beasts have a food-for-pest-control deal that benefits both.

There is also mutualism at work between animals and plant life in the wild. Elephants are herbivores, which means they eat plants. To get enough food, they browse, or select a number of different plants to eat, buffet-style. This causes fairly large areas of vegetation to disappear with each meal. To protect itself from browsing, the African acacia tree has developed a mutualistic relationship with two different species of ant. The tiny ants swarm, or gather in great numbers, around the trunk and limbs of the tree, biting animals that try to browse. In exchange, the ants get fed nectar from the trees' thorns, which are another defense the acacia has against herbivores. The ants also receive a place to live within the tree system.

Humans interact with animals as well, although not always in a mutualistic manner. Domesticated creatures and livestock do experience some mutual benefits from their relationships with humans. They keep humans company, provide protection and transportation, or help with strenuous tasks such as plowing and heavy lifting. In exchange, they receive food, shelter, and affection.

TREATING WILDLIFE AS A NATURAL RESOURCE

Natural resources are materials found in nature that are valuable to whoever owns or controls them. Nonliving items such as timber, oil, coal, and precious metals (gold, silver) are considered the most common natural resources to come from the wilderness. However, there are many ways that animals, too, have been considered a valuable natural resource.

The most obvious example is using wildlife for food. As carnivores, people have been eating animals since prehistoric times. Sometimes, it's not just a case of a hunter shooting a deer and eating the venison. There is a rising market for "exotic" wildlife meat in America, including ostrich, alligator, bear, and bison.

The main trouble with hunting and consuming wildlife is the threat of overkill. Humans have shown a tendency to take more than they need when it comes to hunting wild animals for food. In fact, anthropologists think that cave dwellers, trying to put food on the table, hunted the mastodon and wooly mammoth (ancient species of elephants) into extinction. This is known as overconsumption. Modern hunters have regulations regarding hunting seasons and the number of animals they can kill to help make sure wildlife populations do not disappear completely. Still, people engage in illegal hunting, known as poaching.

It's possible that neither the Ice Age nor a giant meteor killed off the mastodon. Scientists think overhunting might have been the reason for the creature's extinction.

Sometimes, wildlife is hunted not for food but for sport or recreation. In other words, hunters kill for fun or to get a trophy and do not need or use the meat. Sport hunting, as it is called, takes place in the wild but is also permitted in many wildlife refuges, national forests, and state parks, as well as on other public and private land.

Another way wildlife has been used as a resource is in the name of science. Vivisection, a process in which live animals are cut open and examined for scientific purposes, had been a common form of medical research

Wildlife as Moneymakers

Wildlife can also be treated as a natural resource—and a national treasure—in much more positive ways. Bwindi National Park in Uganda charges tourists to visit and observe gorillas and other wild animals in their natural habitat. Around 12 percent of collected entrance fees gets pumped back into the local economy, allowing villagers to understand the value of protecting wildlife and preserving wildlife areas. The same thing is happening all across Africa. In fact, because animals have become a rich source of income and an important natural resource, wildlife has come to be known as the "oil of Kenya."

since the 1500s. These days, doctors and students are more likely to use dissection, in which already dead animals are used for the same research purposes. Yet, live animals are still used in laboratories to test drugs, cosmetics, and medical procedures. The wildlife on which experiments have been, and are being, conducted include a large number of chimpanzees and other primates, which are the species of mammal most closely linked to humans at the genetic level.

Animal-derived products have also been, and currently are being, used as ingredients in medicine. For example, thousands of antibiotics, including penicillin and tetracycline, were originally made from microorganisms that live throughout various ecosystems. Medicines used to treat osteoporosis and control bleeding during open-heart surgery are derived from salmon. Doctors are experimenting with drugs made from snake venom, which they think might slow cancer's growth and help reduce the effects of having a stroke. Other animal parts, such as rhinoceros horns, elephant tusks, and the gallbladders of black bears, are considered medicinal by various cultures.

Wildlife is also considered a source of entertainment and unusual or exotic pets. Animal acts with tigers, lions, bears, and elephants are main attractions at circuses that travel all around the world. Wild animals are trained to "act" in movies and television series. Meanwhile, the market for exotic pets keeps growing, especially in the United States. Many different species are kept as pets around the world, including endangered animals such as gorillas. The International Fund for Animal Welfare estimates that there are twice as many Siberian tigers being kept in people's homes than there are in the wild. If that estimate is correct, then that would mean there are around ten thousand tigers kept as pets. Needless to say, wildlife cannot be domesticated and make bad—and often dangerous—pets.

AT YOUR SERVICE

Animals and plants do not exist simply to fulfill our wants and needs. Every living thing on Earth plays a role in

Concerned about the welfare of circus and other captive show animals, protesters find creative ways to argue that wild creatures deserve to be free.

keeping the planet healthy and able to support life—plants and animals included. In fact, wildlife helps sustain the world's ecosystems much better than humans do. Human actions frequently wind up putting the environment, and wildlife, at great risk.

How wild animals act around other species and the nonliving parts of their habitat directly affects the way the world works. An animal's job is to stay alive. That involves getting food and water and staying safe from diseases and predators. In the process, animals provide what scientists call ecological services, which are actions that positively affect the availability of life's necessities, such as food, water, and shelter, for all living members of an ecosystem. By doing its job, each creature either directly or indirectly maintains or alters its surroundings in such a way that other animals can do their job as well.

Wild animals provide many useful services simply by living the way nature intended them to live. Among these services are cleaning the air and water, making the soil rich enough to grow plants, pollinating crops for food, reducing the number of pests and harmful diseases, and keeping the climate stable.

For instance, there are several invertebrate species that eat the organic waste that collects on the ground, such as dead leaves and other plant life. They then digest it and convert it into nutrients, which in turn are absorbed by plants and trees. By changing waste into nutrients, these creatures feed the vegetation, which then feeds other animals and humans. Birds, bees, and butterflies pollinate, or fertilize, crops, which is an extremely valuable service when you consider that the pollination of flowers is responsible for more than 30 percent of all human food production.

THE DOMINO EFFECT

Ecosystems have been described as an interdependent web of life, with hundreds of delicate threads connecting species to each other and making a mutually beneficial whole. There is some flexibility in this web. It can survive the loss or addition of a species without falling apart. However, if pushed too far by the loss of too much wildlife, enough of the web's interspecies connections will be severed, and the web will break.

Wild populations are so interdependent that even a small change to any one species will have an effect on several other species. This is called the domino effect. It's like lining up a row of domino tiles standing on their ends and gently tipping one tile. That tile hits another, which hits another, until the whole row soon collapses. The domino effect can spell doom for an entire ecosystem.

LESSONS LEARNED IN YELLOWSTONE

A real-life example of the domino effect has occurred in Yellowstone National Park over the last eighty years. Because they were thought to be a danger to park visitors and livestock on nearby ranches, wolf populations in Yellowstone were hunted and killed. They became extinct within the park's boundaries in 1926. Without predator wolves around, populations of their main prey, elk, grew dramatically. That meant many more elk were now foraging in an area that had not changed in size to accommodate them. As a result, large herds began to browse on young cottonwood, aspen, and willow trees, which reduced the number of these trees that were allowed to grow to maturity. Many fruit-bearing shrubs that grew near the banks of rivers and streams alongside these trees were destroyed by grazing as well.

Subsequently, Yellowstone's waterside habitats suffered. The lack of trees left many birds homeless, and the lack of fruit shrubs meant there was less for them to eat as well. Several bird species were left with no choice but to fly elsewhere and find a more suitable habitat. Beavers had no material to build dams, so eventually they, too, left the park. Ponds created by beaver dams disappeared, as did the cold water that flowed from the dams into streams. Without cold-water streams, trout began to struggle to survive. One by one, the park's species became endangered.

In 1995, wolves were brought back to Yellowstone. Since then,

Order was restored to Yellowstone's ecosystem soon after humans reintroduced grey wolves into the park. Federal officials brought the first wolves in via crates.

the park's ecosystem has started to regain its once-healthy balance. The lesson is that biodiversity and balance within an ecosystem are crucial to its survival. The addition or subtraction of any one species, no matter how small or seemingly insignificant, can result in disaster.

Large chunks of the Brazilian rain forest—home to many wildlife species—have been cleared in recent years. Activities such as this threaten habitats and wild animals globally.

Life in the wild has always been dangerous, but never as much as it is today. Wildlife around the globe is under attack like never before. Species are losing their habitats at an alarming rate, and, thanks to overdevelopment and pollution, there are fewer unspoiled wilderness spaces left on which they can build new ones. Shrinking and disappearing habitats have also led to a shortage of food. Animals weakened by hunger are easy targets for the infectious diseases that are spreading through ecosystems like wildfire. Speaking of which, wildfires and other natural disasters are also on the upswing, the result of climate change and global warming.

With all of these threats in place, wildlife must adapt or face extinction. And adaptation isn't always possible. What makes the situation even worse is that overwhelming evidence shows that the main culprit behind the growth of these threats is the human race.

LOSS OF HABITAT

According to figures released by the World Wildlife Fund (WWF), about half of the world's forests have disappeared. The other half is being destroyed ten times faster than it would take an average forest to regrow. We're losing approximately 50,193 square miles (130,000 square kilometers) of tropical forests, such as the Amazon rain forest, each year. That's roughly the size of forty-two American football fields. A 2007 study showed that more than half of forty-nine island countries surveyed are engaged in overfishing, which also contributes to the loss of the oceans' coral reef habitats.

This is just a very small sample of the habitat loss occurring today. With each instance of damage to an ecosystem or habitat comes the loss of a great deal of wildlife. In fact, habitat loss is the biggest reason wildlife species become extinct. Without the food, water, and shelter habitats provide, no species can exist.

Habitat loss can occur in one of three ways: complete loss, fragmentation, or degradation. A complete loss is when an entire habitat is destroyed. The plants, animals, and nonliving surroundings are eliminated completely from an area. Fragmentation is when a terrestrial ecosystem is cut up into fragments, or smaller habitats that are not physically connected to each other. Fragmentation is especially tough on large predators, which need wide, uninterrupted hunting areas. Degradation is when a habitat is spoiled to the point that it can no longer sustain life. The habitat's environment becomes toxic, or poisonous and harmful, to wildlife because of unnatural influences such as pollution.

DEVELOPMENT

Habitat loss can occur naturally because of fire, flood, or other natural disaster. Habitat degradation can result from organic litter and sedimentation, which is natural waste matter that accumulates and settles at the bottom of lakes, streams, and rivers. Most of the time, though, habitat loss and degradation are the result of human activity, such as development.

In this case, the definition of development is to change or add to an area of land or water in an attempt to get the most value out of it. The reason humans develop more and more land is overpopulation. The number of people on Earth keeps growing by millions each year. All these people need a place to live, but there's a limited amount of space in which they can do that.

FARMING AND URBAN SPRAWL

Agriculture is one of the primary forms of land development. Humans' ever-increasing need for food has resulted in great areas of wilderness being cleared to create farms. Clearing means getting rid of trees and plants so land can be used for other purposes. In this case, the purpose for the land is still to grow plants, except that the plants are now crops that humans can eat, rather than those eaten by wildlife. Agricultural crops are not as efficient and powerful carbon dioxide absorbers as trees and wilderness vegetation are, so agricultural development actually contributes to global warming and climate change, which further compromises habitats and ecosystems. In addition, when livestock graze in fields instead of wildlife making their homes in wilderness, habitat is lost and the food supply for wild animals is reduced.

Farms and houses tend to squeeze wildlife out of their habitats. This kind of development can destroy the necessary biodiversity found in nature.

Clearing of land also occurs when humans build homes, offices, shopping malls, and other buildings. When all the available land in one area has been developed, building usually branches out to nearby plots of vacant land. Construction of new homes, shopping malls, office complexes, and highways that spills over from cities and towns into wilderness areas is referred to as urban sprawl.

Three American environmental groups—the National Wildlife Federation, Smart Growth America, and

NatureServe—issued a report in 2005 that identified the thirty-five fastest-growing urban areas in the United States. These expanding localities are expected to gobble up more than 22,000 acres (8,900 hectares) of wildlife habitat for development by the year 2030. The majority of this damaging urban sprawl is expected to occur near major cities in California, but towns in Nevada, southern Florida, and parts of Alabama should also be affected.

LOGGING AND MINING

Other human activities have obliterated, fragmented, or degraded habitats as well. Logging has been, and continues to be, the main reason for habitat loss in tropical forests. Scientists say tropical forests are ecosystems that contain more than half of Earth's species. Cutting down trees to use as lumber—typically to build houses or furniture and make paper products for human use—leaves animals, especially birds, without homes or protection. Also, taking away a large number of trees loosens the soil enough to cause erosion, which is when land and valuable soil are swept away by rain or wind. Erosion causes sedimentation, which degrades natural water resources and negatively affects fish, aquatic plant species, and other forms of marine life.

Mining leaves huge, permanent craters in the land and, in the process, destroys the water and soil surrounding these pits.

Mining occurs when humans want to access natural resources, such as oil and minerals, which are buried deep within the soil. This means digging into the earth and not only disrupting wildlife habitats, but also leaving deep scars in the land that may never heal. The dirt, rocks, and plants that are removed to create mines are treated as waste products, and the mining process creates pollution that spoils the remaining habitats' food and water resources.

CLIMATE CHANGE AND HABITAT LOSS

With development comes a lot of pollution, especially increased amounts of toxic fumes, or emissions, from cars, trucks, and other motorized equipment. Emissions created by fossil fuels like gasoline, oil, and coal have been tied to a weather-related phenomenon known as

Tigers vs. Talc

There are only three thousand Indian tigers left in the wild, a relatively low number that has placed the animal high on the world's endangered species list. Now, the remaining tigers living in supposedly safe habitats called sanctuaries and reserves near Delhi are facing a new threat—from the cosmetics counter of your favorite store.

In addition to being home to tiger reserves, the Indian state of Rajasthan also happens to be rich in soapstone and marble. These are the source materials of talcum powder, a common ingredient found in cosmetics and toiletry items. Talc is used in everything from eye shadow to deodorant. Illegal mining operations have sprung up throughout the tigers' sanctuaries. The mining ravages what is supposed to be protected habitat and leaves the Indian tiger at an even greater risk of extinction.

global warming, which the world currently is experiencing. Gases such as carbon dioxide linger in the atmosphere and trap heat from the sun. The result is that temperatures on Earth rise—not by much, but enough to create climate change. In addition to rising temperatures, global warming can result in a greater frequency and intensity of all sorts of weather-related problems and natural disasters, including hurricanes, droughts, fires, and floods.

Scientists have discovered a strong link between climate change and endangered wildlife species. Global warming causes a number of problems with wildlife habitats. Rising sea levels, brought on by melting polar ice and increased levels of precipitation, swamp the habitats of some animals, including the shoreline nesting grounds of sea turtles. Hurricanes and wildfires damage and obliterate, or totally destroy, areas that wildlife call home.

Studies indicate that higher temperatures have caused cold-weather terrestrial and marine animals to move northward in search of cooler habitats. Researchers have noticed that even fish in the chilly waters of the North Sea have started moving farther north as water temperatures rise. The trouble is that wildlife already living in northern habitats don't have anywhere else to go. They're stuck in a habitat that is changing before their eyes.

The ability of species to gather food and give birth is threatened by climate change. Shorter winters throw wildlife's timing off to the point that there is a mismatch between feeding periods and the availability of food. For example, polar bears in the Canadian Arctic are losing weight because warmer temperatures make the ice of their hunting grounds melt earlier than usual, so they miss out on several weeks of hunting each spring. The weight loss doesn't just make the bears skinnier. It also affects females' ability to get pregnant and have healthy cubs.

INVASIVE SPECIES

According to officials at the Smithsonian National Zoological Park in Washington, D.C., invasive species are the second-leading cause of endangerment and extinction, after habitat loss. Invasive species are intruders. They are animals that wind up in an area where they are not normally found.

Most invasive species are introduced to an alien habitat as the result of human-related activity. For instance, some forms of shellfish and other marine animals attach themselves to the bottom of cargo ships bringing goods across the ocean. Insects and small mammals or amphibians may accidentally stow away in shipping crates or travelers' luggage. Still others are brought to a foreign habitat on purpose by people who want to keep wild animals as pets. Too many times, owners release exotic pets and birds into a wilderness area near their homes when they grow tired of the animals or can no longer take care of them. People mistakenly believe that because the creature is wild to begin with, it will automatically adapt to any wilderness habitat.

Invasive species are a threat to native, or naturally belonging, species mainly because the more animals in any habitat, the more competition there is for space, food, and water. Some invasive species are stronger than native dwellers, or they may be natural predators of certain native species, so they often win the battle for habitat.

DISEASE

Another threat from invasive species is the danger of disease they pose. When pets and wild animals are shipped from one country to another, they normally have to go through quarantine. This is a period of time when an animal is kept away from other animals and humans to make sure it does not pass on any infectious diseases. Wildlife that enters a country by accident or through smuggling does not go through this process, and these animals may carry diseases with them.

Invasive species are not the only animals that can threaten wildlife with disease. Because the loss of habitat has put them in closer proximity, wildlife can also contract diseases from domestic animals and livestock. For instance, foot-and-mouth disease is an infection that is shared among hoofed livestock (cows, horses) and wildlife (deer, moose). It has occasionally plagued places like Canada and England for many years.

Some diseases can cause outbreaks that either significantly reduce populations of a species or wipe them out altogether. In Tasmania, scientists are seeing an outbreak of a facial tumor disease that has killed nearly half of all the world's Tasmanian devils in the last three years. These devils are mammals found only in Tasmania.

Scientists are now concerned that certain diseases found in wildlife may be transmitted to humans. In 2008, an international research team determined that more than half the world's emerging diseases (diseases that are either new or have moved into new regions) traveled from animals to humans. Most of those, such as HIV/AIDS (originating in chimps) and SARS (from bats) came from wildlife-human interaction.

Zoologists are fighting to save the rare Tasmanian devil from the effects of a disfiguring and deadly illness. Diseases threaten many animals around the world.

Sea turtles are struggling to get off the endangered species list. They are being helped toward this goal by conservation efforts that protect their aquatic habitat and beach nesting grounds.

One in four mammals, one in every three amphibians, and one in eight birds in the world are currently in danger of extinction. There are close to six hundred scientifically determined "hot spots" on the planet, where hundreds of rare species exist under the constant and very real threat of losing their habitat. Many of these hot spots are surrounded by human communities that get bigger every year because of a population explosion.

What are we humans, one of the biggest threats wildlife has ever known, doing to save the world's ecosystems and their endangered animal inhabitants? Steps are being taken. Many organizations and dedicated individuals work hard to conserve and preserve various species, keeping them alive and healthy. Yet it's a difficult battle, one in which the rewards are not always immediate.

There are two things humans need to do in order to save wildlife: preserve the animals and ecosystems that are still around, and change or halt the activities that cause harm in the first place.

CONSERVATION

Saving wildlife doesn't happen by chance. It starts with a plan. Wildlife conservation involves studying species and their needs, investigating what resources are available, then finding ways to apply these resources to habitat preservation and wildlife protection. Sometimes called wildlife management, conservation is performed by zoologists—scientists who study animals—biologists, and environmentalists.

It is important to remember that citizens of many poorer countries often don't have the option of helping wildlife. They have to help themselves first. For these

Losses That Are Too Hot to Handle

First identified in the 1980s, biodiversity "hot spots" are places on Earth that have populations of plants and animals that can be found nowhere else but that are also experiencing dangerous habitat losses. These twenty-five locations cover less than 2 percent of Earth's total land mass but contain more than half of the world's terrestrial biodiversity.

Hot spots can be found on every continent but Antarctica. The hottest of the hot spots are in Tanzania, Kenya, the Philippines, and Polynesia-Micronesia. Although it only has one hot spot—California's Floristic Province—the United States ranks second on the 2007 International Union for the Conservation of Nature and Natural Resource's "Red List" of top countries for endangered species.

people, the only land available for farming may be wildlife habitat. In some communities, there aren't many jobs available, so people have to hunt and fish to keep their families fed.

Some people, especially those in underdeveloped nations, need to be convinced that saving animal species from extinction is worth their while. That is why it is important to include local communities in any decisions concerning wildlife management. Conservation efforts cannot succeed without "buy-in" from people sharing an ecosystem with animals.

A number of wild species can call game reserves their home. These areas have to cover a lot of space to accommodate large, widely grazing animals such as giraffes.

PROTECTED AREAS

Protection is a huge factor in wildlife conservation. In order to conserve species and maintain the largest possible amount of biodiversity, humans need to protect animals from threats such as habitat loss, overconsumption and overhunting, and development. Often, the best and easiest way to do that is to set aside places in terrestrial and aquatic ecosystems that are meant to be

This red-shouldered hawk seems to be reminding everyone that the wildlife in national parks is protected by government rules and regulations.

used by wildlife only, with minimal or no interference from people.

Among the world's protected areas are national parks, which exist on every continent except Antarctica. A safe haven for many different types of plants and animals, national parks are created and maintained by the governments of each country where they are located. Several countries, including the United States, dedicate entire departments of their governments to managing these parks. Areas known as wildlife reserves, preserves, or refuges operate a lot like national parks, only they are run by state governments or as privately owned businesses.

According to the National Parks Conservation Association, practically one-third of endangered and threatened species in America live within U.S. national park boundaries. Hunting, fishing, and development are either forbidden or greatly restricted in national parks. Development includes not only building but mining and logging as well. People who want to visit these parks have to follow strict guidelines, and campers have to get a permit.

The United States also has national marine protected areas (MPAs), which act as national parks or reserves in water ecosystems. Other countries have similar protected aquatic areas, but they call them different names, such as "particularly sensitive sea areas." As with national parks and land conservation areas, MPAs also have restrictions on fishing, mining for oil and gas, and tourism. Wildlife that live in wetlands, which are habitats formed where land meets water (like swamps and bogs), also receive similar protection.

While such areas offer protection, they are not a perfect solution to the threat of endangerment or extinction. Protected areas often fall victim to pollution that travels in on the wind and in streams flowing from sources outside their control. Unfortunately, illegal hunting, fishing, mining, and logging are common occurrences in reserves and parks as well. The cities, towns, ranches, and farms that surround these safe spots also increase the chances of wildlife-human interactions, as animals wander across boundaries and into places that may be harmful to them.

As you can see, conservation efforts alone will not save some species from extinction. To really make a difference, people have to be willing to make some adaptations of their own.

SUSTAINABLE DEVELOPMENT

Humans think of development as changing the environment for the better by adding lots of stuff to it that increases its entertainment, retail, economic, or convenience value. The problem is that what's added, like roads and houses, is beneficial only to humans. For wildlife, it's a disaster. As increased development leads to the endangerment and extinction of more and more species, ecosystems will change for the worse. Without a healthy ecosystem and the wildlife services we've come to depend upon, people will suffer as well. So, in the long run, overdevelopment also hurts the species it was supposed to help—humans.

Likewise, it wouldn't be practical to leave all wilderness completely untouched. Forbidding humans to develop ecosystems for their use would deny them food, water, shelter, room to interact, and a way to earn a living. These are the basic necessities for human survival.

Finding a balance between the need for wildlife and human habitats, then, is very important. To accomplish this, environmentalists have proposed a compromise form of development, in which people are able to build upon their surroundings and support themselves without using up natural resources and endangering wild animals. It's a concept first started in the 1980s called sustainable development.

Using "green," or environmentally sound, building materials helps make sustainable development possible. Here, builders incorporate solar roof panels and light-attracting plants to heat a home naturally.

Based on the idea that you don't take more than you need from the environment, sustainable development is an attempt to let humans help themselves while also protecting the planet. Planning how to use land in a way that is least destructive to wildlife habitats might include steps such as:

- Rerouting a road so it doesn't cause habitat fragmentation

- Building up (high-rises, multiple-level parking garages) instead of out (urban sprawl)
- Redeveloping run-down or vacated properties, instead of simply building new ones
- Making an agreement with nearby towns and villages that consolidate, or share, resources such as water, energy, and waste removal
- Using environmentally friendly materials (recycled lumber, solar panels) to build with
- Landscaping residential neighborhoods and business parks with native plant species

FARMING WITH A CONSCIENCE

The ways in which humans grow crops and raise livestock for food have a direct effect on wildlife survival. Poor land use, pollution from pesticides and chemical fertilizers, and damming a river to water crops are all human activities that threaten the lives of wild animals. That is why educational institutions such as Auburn University and the University of Georgia have teamed up with the National Aeronautics and Space Administration (NASA) to develop farming methods that make money for farmers while still protecting the environment.

Precision agriculture is better farming through technology. Satellites and aerial photographs are used to get a better idea of how well crops are spaced, to make sure they have room to grow while using the land wisely. Satellite and aerial photos can also provide information about crop and soil health. Global positioning sensors (GPS) and thermal indicators help pinpoint areas that need to be fertilized and watered.

Water Deficit Index (WDI), 24 June 1994
Maricopa Agricultural Center, Arizona

0.0   WDI   1.0

Satellite photography shows farmers how to best care for their crops. The colored grids indicate where in the fields water is needed the most.

Humans can also help salvage habitats and biodiversity without using a lot of gadgets. Organic farming doesn't use chemical pesticides, fertilizers, or other additives. Farmers rely on natural means and products to get rid of pests, grow large crops, and feed livestock. Organic agriculture reduces the risk of pollution and harmful chemicals degrading wildlife habitats that are located near farms.

This type of farming is also becoming more profitable as its popularity with consumers skyrockets. People are becoming more aware of human threats to the environment and, as a result, are choosing a more natural, "green" lifestyle. Organic food is the greener choice, so more consumers are demanding this type of merchandise, even though it costs a little bit more. Organics are good for the environment, wildlife and its habitats, the humans who produce them, and the folks who eat them. Everybody wins when humans go organic.

THE REDUCTION OF GREENHOUSE GASES

Human-generated greenhouse gases—called that because they trap heat on Earth like the windows of a greenhouse keep heat inside to warm plants—are the main cause of global warming. Reducing the amount of these gases—particularly the carbon dioxide emitted when fossil fuels are burned—in the atmosphere would go a long way toward keeping wildlife, and even people, safe from harm.

There are a number of ways to reduce greenhouse gases. Researchers all over the world are investigating new environmentally friendly technology and energy sources that don't emit dangerous fumes or pollute the environment. Hybrid cars that operate on a combination of battery and gas power are a good example of this. Driving less, turning off lights and other electronics when not in use, and recycling are all things individuals can do to reduce their personal emissions of greenhouse gases.

One of the best methods of reducing carbon emissions is to leave ecosystems alone and not disturb existing habitats (which includes not turning wilderness areas into farm or grazing land). Trees and wild plants filter carbon dioxide, the most common and dangerous greenhouse gas, out of the air. The more plant species, the less buildup of harmful carbon dioxide.

WHAT YOU CAN DO

Most of the conservation ideas discussed in this chapter are actions that can be taken by communities, governments, and industry. There are also steps you can take, as an individual, to lessen the threat to Earth's wildlife.

First and foremost, you can respect all life, including the lives of wild animals. Let it show in everything you say and do. When you are camping or just taking a walk or bike ride in the wilderness, try not to disturb any wild animals or plants you come across. It's OK to watch from a distance for a while, but remember, you are in their home. Act the same way you would like guests to treat your home. That also includes leaving the habitat as you found it. Don't litter, and try not to leave behind any other signs that you were in the area. This is what environmentalists mean when they talk about "leave no trace."

Finally, since wild animals cannot talk (at least not in a way that humans can understand), they need you to speak for them. Become a wildlife advocate. Write letters to the editor of your local newspaper about endangered wildlife and why these animals and habitats are worth saving. Tell your state and federal government representatives, by phone or letter, that you'd appreciate their support for legislation that helps preserve local ecosystems and habitats. Consider giving your time and money to an organization that supports wildlife causes.

No one knows for sure if these and other actions will be enough to save wildlife from the extreme threat of extinction. Only time will tell. But given how inter-dependent all forms of life are upon this Earth, our own survival may depend upon the preservation of our animal counterparts and their natural habitats.

GLOSSARY

adaptation Getting used to something, or changing so that a given situation better fits your needs.

biodiversity The number and variety of species found within an ecosystem.

camouflage To hide or conceal by blending in with your environment.

commodity Something useful that can be traded, usually for money.

conservation The saving of something from loss, damage, or neglect.

degradation A decline in the condition; spoiled to the point of not being able to sustain life.

domesticated Trained or adapted to live in a human-controlled environment.

domino effect Occurrence in which even a small change to any one member of a community has an effect on several others in a chain reaction.

fragmentation When a terrestrial ecosystem is cut up into fragments, or smaller habitats that are not physically connected to each other.

habitat A place to live that provides the basic necessities, such as food, water, and shelter.

hot spots Places on Earth containing plants and animals that can't be found anywhere else but that are also experiencing dangerous habitat losses.

invasive species An intruder; alien species.

migrate To move to a different location from time to time, especially as the seasons change.

mimicry The act of copying or imitating; when an animal fools predators into thinking it is stronger and better able to defend itself by looking like another, similar, more threatening animal.

mutualistic When species of wildlife interact with and support each other for the benefit of all.

native Having a long, multigenerational history of existing in or belonging to a certain ecosystem.

obliterate To totally destroy.

predator A species that survives by hunting, killing, and eating smaller and weaker creatures.

sustainable development When people are able to build upon their surroundings and support themselves without using up natural resources and endangering wildlife.

terrestrial On land.

toxic Poisonous; harmful to health.

FOR MORE INFORMATION

National Wildlife Federation (NWF)
11100 Wildlife Center Drive
Reston, VA 20190-5362
(800) 822-9919
Web site: http://www.nwf.org
The NWF seeks to confront the issue of global warming
and its effect on wildlife, protect and restore wildlife
habitat, and connect the next generation of
Americans to nature.

Nature Canada
85 Albert Street, Suite 900
Ottawa, ON K1P 6A4
Canada
(800) 267-4088
Web site: http://www.naturecanada.ca
Through community-based efforts, advocacy, outreach,
and education, Nature Canada protects nature, its
diversity, and the processes that sustain it.

The Nature Conservancy
4245 North Fairfax Drive, Suite 100
Arlington, VA 22203-1606
(703) 841-5300
Web site: http://www.nature.org

The Nature Conservancy is a leading conservation organization that works around the world to protect important lands and waters.

World Wildlife Fund (WWF)
1250 24th Street NW
P.O. Box 97180
Washington, DC 20090-7180
(202) 293-4800
Web site: http://www.worldwildlife.org
WWF's mission is the conservation of nature. Using the best available scientific knowledge, WWF works to preserve the diversity and abundance of life on Earth and the health of ecological systems.

WEB SITES

Due to the changing nature of Internet links, Rosen Publishing has developed an online list of Web sites related to the subject of this book. This site is updated regularly. Please use this link to access this list:

http://www.rosenlinks.com/eet/enwi

For Further Reading

Arnold, Caroline. *El Niño: Stormy Weather for People and Wildlife*. New York, NY: Clarion Books, 2005.

Chinery, Michael. *Animal Habitats*. London, England: Southwater, 2002.

Fothergill, Alistair, and David Attenborough. *Planet Earth: As You've Never Seen It Before*. Berkeley, CA: University of California Press, 2007.

Garbuny Vogel, Carole. *Ocean Wildlife (The Restless Sea)*. Danbury, CT: Franklin Watts, 2003.

McGavin, George C. *Endangered: Wildlife on the Brink of Extinction*. New York, NY: Firefly Books, 2006.

Pearce, Q. L. *James Quadrino: Wildlife Protector*. Chicago, IL: KidHaven Press, 2006.

Petersen, Christine. *Conservation*. Danbury, CT: Children's Press, 2004.

Taylor, Barbara. *Bugs and Minibeasts*. London, England: Southwater, 2003.

BIBLIOGRAPHY

Barnett, Antony. "West's Love of Talc Threatens India's Tigers." *Observer* (London), June 22, 2003, News section, p. 8.

Blakslee, Sandra. "In Tasmania, the Devil Now Faces Its Own Hell." *New York Times*, May 31, 2005, Vol. 154, Issue 53231, pp. F1–F4.

Canadian Forest Congress. "Carbon Capture, Water Filtration, Other Boreal Forest Ecoservices Worth Estimated $250 Billion/Year." *ScienceDaily*, September 2006. Retrieved March 2008 (http://www.sciencedaily.com/releases/2006/09/060924175538.htm).

Dilworth, David J. "Ecological Interdependence." Helping Our Peninsula's Environment (HOPE). Retrieved March 2008 (http://www.1hope.org/intdpndt.htm).

Goodman, Steven J., and Doug Rickman. "Precision Agriculture." NASA, October 1999. Retrieved April 2008 (http://www.ghcc.msfc.nasa.gov/precisionag).

Markey, Sean. "Polar Bears Suffering as Arctic Summers Come Earlier, Study Finds." *National Geographic News*, September 2006. Retrieved March 2008 (http://news.nationalgeographic.com/news/2006/09/060921-polar-bears.html).

Moyle, Peter, and Mary A. Orland. "A History of Wildlife in North America." MarineBio.org, July 2004.

Retrieved March 2008 (http://marinebio.org/
Oceans/Conservation/Moyle/ch2.asp).

Stauth, David. "Scientists: Wolves Helping Rebalance
Yellowstone Ecosystem." Oregon State University
News & Communication Services, October 2003.
Retrieved March 2008 (http://oregonstate.edu/dept/
ncs/newsarch/2003/Oct03/wolf.htm).

Towson University Center for GIS. "What Are the
Effects?: Habitat Degradation, Loss, and
Fragmentation." *Chesapeake Bay & Mid-Atlantic
from Space*. Retrieved March 2008 (http://
chesapeake.towson.edu/landscape/impervious/
all_habitat.asp).

University of California–Santa Barbara. "Biodiversity
Controls Ecological 'Services,' Report Scientists in
Comprehensive Analysis." *ScienceDaily*, November
2006. Retrieved March 2008 (http://www.sciencedaily.
com/releases/2006/10/061025185158.htm).

Woodhouse, Mark E. J. "Epidemiology: Emerging
Diseases Go Global." *Nature*, Issue 7181, Vol. 451,
February 21, 2008, pp. 898–899.

World Wildlife Fund. "Losing Their Homes Because of
the Growing Needs of Humans." Retrieved March
2008 (http://www.panda.org/about_wwf/what_we_
do/species/problems/habitat_loss_degradation/
index.cfm).

INDEX

ABOUT THE AUTHOR

Jeanne Nagle is a writer and editor in upstate New York. She has a longstanding interest in environmental issues and is a member of Care of God's Creation, a grassroots environmental group in her area. Among her many titles for Rosen Publishing are *Reducing Your Carbon Footprint at School*, *Smart Shopping: Shopping Green*, and *In the News: Living Green*.

PHOTO CREDITS

Cover © www.istockphoto.com/Jan Will; pp. 1, 11, 42 © National Geographic/Getty Images; pp. 4–5 © www.istockphoto.com/Rich Phatin; p. 8 © Tim Graham/Getty Images; p. 14 © Biosphoto/Klein j.-L. & Hubert M.L./Peter Arnold, Inc.; pp. 15, 26, 29, 45 © AFP/Getty Images; p. 17 © www.istockphoto.com/Michel De Nijs; p. 19 © Bildarchiv Preussicher Kulturbesitz/Art Resource; p. 21 © Martin Harvey/Peter Arnold; p. 23 © Julie Dermansky/Photo Researchers; pp. 30, 41, 46 © Getty Images; p. 34 © AP Photos; p. 36 © www.istockphoto.com/Rob Broek; p. 49 © www.istockphoto.com/Jim Pruitt; p. 51 USDA.

Designer: Tom Forget; Photo Researcher: Marty Levick